ideals

EASTER ISSUE

May the wondrous Easter story
Thrill your soul with hope anew,
Bringing all God's richest blessings
In the springtime just for you . . .

May your faith again be strengthened
Through the cross upon the hill,
And the glorious resurrection
All its promises fulfill . . .

So on this glad Easter morning
May God's love enfold your heart,
Offer grace in deepest measure
Which this season does impart.

Marian L. Moore

editor
Maryjane Hooper Tonn

•

managing editor
Lorraine Obst

•

assistant managing editor
Ralph Luedtke

associate editor
Charles Roberts

IDEALS—Vol. 32, No. 2—March, MCMLXXV. Published bimonthly by IDEALS PUBLISHING CORP., 11315 Watertown Plank Road, Milwaukee, Wis. 53226. Second-class postage paid at Milwaukee, Wisconsin. Copyright © MCMLXXV by IDEALS PUBLISHING CORP. All rights reserved. Title IDEALS registered U.S. Patent Office.
ONE YEAR SUBSCRIPTION—six consecutive issues as published—only $8.50
TWO YEAR SUBSCRIPTION—twelve consecutive issues as published—only $16.00
SINGLE ISSUES—only $2.25

John Gadja

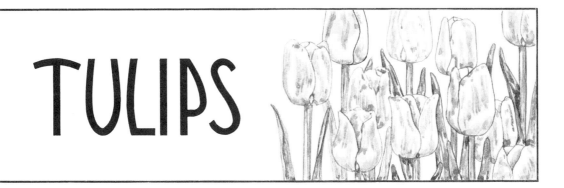

TULIPS

Neath late October's bright, warm sun,
The happy Autumn work's begun.

The bulbs are tucked within the earth
To wait till springtime gives them birth.

Five months go by and winter's snow
Protects the sleeping bulbs below.

In March they push up brownish spears,
Then flare out leaves like rabbit ears!

Then tall and stately stems arise,
As gentle rain falls from the skies.

Mid-April sees their cups unfold . . .
The pink, the scarlet, white and gold!

What beauty glows in every cup,
When tulips lift each chalice up!

J. Harold Gwynne

The Coming of Spring

There's something in the air
That's new and sweet and rare...
A scent of springtime things,
A whir as if of wings.

There's something, too, that's new
In the color of the blue
That's in the morning sky,
Before the sun is high.

And though on plain and hill
'Tis winter, winter still,
There's something seems to say
That winter's had its day...

And all this changing tint,
This whispering stir and hint
Of bud and bloom and wing,
Is the coming of the spring.

And tomorrow or today
The brooks will break away
From their icy, frozen sleep,
And run and laugh and leap.

And the next thing in the woods,
The catkins in their hoods
Of fur and silk will stand,
A sturdy little band.

And the tassels soft and fine
Of the hazel will entwine,
And the elder branches show
Their buds against the snow.

So, silently but swift,
Above the wintry drift,
The long days gain and gain,
Until on hill and plain

Once more, and yet once more,
Returning as before,
We see the bloom of birth
Make young again the earth.

Nora Perry

Spring

Wilma Dykeman

That night in late winter when the first peepers call in icy ponds and hidden swamplands, that night marks the first moment of spring.

Old-timers in the mountains say that the first frogs "will look through glass windows three times before spring really breaks," but it is easy to accept three more veils of ice, knowing that those noisy little harbingers are laying their masses of eggs and the new life of spring is stirring under the frozen crust.

After those first frogs, spring seems to rush forth on all fronts. Full streams tumble clear and cold out of the hills where winter snow and rain have made the spongy earth a reservoir of moisture soaked against days of heat and drought to come. Tall stems of trillium and jack-in-the-pulpit thrust up almost overnight. Suddenly, birds are busy everywhere — cardinal, catbird, crow, resident blue jay and migrating grosbeak, and then one moonlit night the mockingbird sings.

Continued

*Photograph opposite
SPRING PLOWING
Black Forest, Germany
Photo – Plessner International*

Spring, like autumn, is a season for bypaths and side roads. The wide highways unrolling across our country are alluring enough, the thoroughfares and turnpikes save time, but occasionally it is good to turn aside from the new concrete ribbons, the easiest route, the quickest way, and follow old gravel roads and country lanes.

Perhaps that is what the simple life anywhere consists of: a momentary turning aside, a glimpse down a different path to see, hear, feel, ponder the uniqueness that is common to our lives.

On side roads wait the little farms, new lambs, new ground, pungent with the smell of fresh roots. You find pastures, too, with salt licks for cattle, abandoned orchards where gnarled old apple trees put forth hopeful bloom. Then there are the deep woods, inviting longer exploration, yielding themselves slowly to the stranger's probing. And all along the way — people — those who will share a moment or an hour in joking, remembering, denouncing, confiding.

Spring approaches — around us, within us. We may turn the new ground of untried appreciation, discover the salt of humor, the gnarled strength of old ideals, the variety of new ideas. There are old friendships whose roots may be strengthened and new friendships to be brought to blossom.

Spring is for sowing good seed, plowing fresh furrows.

An Easter Carol

Spring bursts today, for Christ is risen
 and all the earth's at play.

Flash forth, thou sun, the rain is over
 and gone, its work is done.

Winter is past, sweet spring is come
 at last, is come at last.

Bud, fig and vine, bud, olive, fat
 with fruit and oil, and wine.

Break forth this morn in roses,
 thou but yesterday a thorn.

Uplift thy head, O pure white lily
 through the winter dead.

Beside your dams leap and rejoice,
 you merry-making lambs.

All herds and flocks rejoice, all beasts
 of thickets and of rocks.

Sing, creatures, sing, angels and men
 and birds, and everything.

Christina G. Rossetti

Photograph opposite
CONGREGATIONAL CHURCH
Wethersfield, Connecticut
Photo – Alpha

Tell Me the Stories of Jesus

Tell me the stories of Jesus
    I love to hear;
Things I would ask Him to tell me
    If He were here;
  Scenes by the wayside,
    Tales of the sea,
  Stories of Jesus,
    Tell them to me.

First let me hear how the children
    Stood round His knee,
And I shall fancy His blessing
    Resting on me:
  Words full of kindness,
    Deeds full of grace,
  All in the lovelight
    Of Jesus' face.

Into the city I'd follow
    The children's band,
Waving a branch of the palm tree
    High in my hand;
  One of His heralds,
    Yes, I would sing
  Loudest hosannas,
    Jesus is King!

Tell me, in accents of wonder,
    How rolled the sea
Tossing the boat in a tempest
    On Galilee!
  And how the Master,
    Ready and kind,
  Chided the billows
    And hushed the wind.

Tell how the sparrow that twitters
    On yonder tree,
And the sweet meadow-side lily
    May speak to me:
  Give me their message,
    For I would hear
  How Jesus taught us
    Our Father's care.

Show me that scene in the garden
    Of bitter pain;
And of the Cross where my Saviour
    For me was slain.
  Sad ones or bright ones,
    So that they be
  Stories of Jesus,
    Tell them to me.

William Henry Parker

The Easter Story

Alinari-Scala

Verily, verily, I say unto you,
That ye shall weep and lament,
but the world shall rejoice; and
ye shall be sorrowful, but your
sorrow shall be turned into joy.

St. John 16:20

From Nazareth He Comes

From Nazareth He comes, the carpenter
Who knows of hammering and blows that break
The worker's hands. From Galilee He comes,
The fisherman who walks upon the lake.

Through fields of harvest, ripe for plucking grain,
Along the dusty roads that go beside
The vineyards, Christ, the noble carpenter,
Goes to the city to be crucified.

Jerusalem's streets are filled with those
Who cry "Hosanna!" and others, "Crucify!"
For all of these He hangs upon the cross
That lifts itself into the purple sky.

For all of these the Master lived and died . . .
His lamp is tall and bright; our lamps are dim,
But we can see the way ahead of us,
For where the Master goes we go with Him.

Raymond Kresensky

CHRIST RIDING INTO JERUSALEM
Albert Cuyp, Dutch, 1620-1691

His Last Week

Sunday, the shout of hosannas,
The triumph of palms in Jerusalem.

Friday, the cross on Golgotha,
The mocking of thorns in a diadem.

Highest to lowest, in only a five day span;
Hailed Son of God, and made the derision of man.

Sunday again, and the grave, and the seal
   strangely broken,
And those who had doubted remembering words
   He had spoken.

Elinor Lennen

And they come to Jerusalem: and Jesus went into the temple, and began to cast out them that sold and bought in the temple, and overthrew the tables of the money changers, and the seats of them that sold doves; And would not suffer that any man should carry any vessel through the temple. And he taught, saying unto them, Is it not written, My house shall be called of all nations the house of prayer? but ye have made it a den of thieves.

St. Mark 11:15-17

Lord of Us All

Lord of the strong, when earth you trod,
You calmly faced the angry sea,
The fierce, unmasked hypocrisy,
    The traitor's kiss, the rabble's hiss,
The awful death upon the tree:
    All glory be to God.

Lord of the weak, when earth you trod,
Oppressors writhed beneath your scorn;
The weak, despised, depraved, forlorn,
    You taught to hope and know the scope
Of love divine for all who mourn:
    All glory be to God.

Lord of the rich, when earth you trod,
To Mammon's power you never bowed,
But taught how men with wealth endowed
    In meekness' school might learn to rule
The demon that enslaves the proud:
    All glory be to God.

Lord of the poor, when earth you trod,
The lot you chose was hard and poor;
You taught us hardness to endure,
    And so to gain through hurt and pain
The wealth that lasts forevermore:
    All glory be to God.

Lord of us all, when earth you trod,
The life you led was perfect, free,
Defiant of all tyranny:
    Now give us grace that we may face
Our foes with like temerity,
    And glory give to God.

Donald Hankey

Painting opposite
JESUS DRIVING THE MONEY CHANGER
OUT OF THE TEMPLE
Carl Heinrich Bloch
Danish, 1834-1890
Photo – Three Lions, Inc.

THE LAST SUPPER
Andreas H. Hunaeus
Danish, nineteenth century

The Last Supper

Now when the eventide was come,
With shadows deepening into gloom,
Came Jesus with the twelve and sat
At supper in the upper room.

A solemn hush fell over them,
And in the soft gold candlelight,
His heart was heavy, for He knew
His hour was near at hand that night.

And while they ate, He reverently
Began to bless and break the bread,
"This is My body given for you;
Take ye and eat," the Master said.

He took the cup and giving thanks
He gave it to them lovingly.
"This is My blood, drink ye of it;
Do this in memory of Me."

They would remember all their lives
The poignant beauty in His face,
And treasure, too, the blessed words
He spoke there in that quiet place.

William Arnette Wofford

Then cometh Jesus with them unto a place called Gethsemane, and saith unto the disciples, Sit ye here, while I go and pray yonder. And he took with him Peter and the two sons of Zebedee, and began to be sorrowful and very heavy. Then saith he unto them, My soul is exceeding sorrowful, even unto death: tarry ye here, and watch with me. And he went a little further, and fell on his face, and prayed, saying, O my Father, if it be possible, let this cup pass from me: nevertheless, not as I will, but as thou wilt.

St. Matthew 26:36-39

And the multitude crying aloud began to desire him to do as he had ever done unto them. But Pilate answered them, saying, Will ye that I release unto you the King of the Jews? For he knew that the chief priests had delivered him for envy. But the chief priests moved the people, that he should rather release Barabbas unto them. And Pilate answered and said again unto them, What will ye then that I shall do unto him whom ye call the King of the Jews? And they cried out again, Crucify him. Then Pilate said unto them, Why, what evil hath he done? And they cried out the more exceedingly, Crucify him. And so Pilate, willing to content the people, released Barabbas unto them, and delivered Jesus, when he had scourged him, to be crucified.

St. Mark 15:8-15

At the Cross of Jesus

There is love at the cross of Jesus,
   an everlasting love
That could leave the courts of Heaven
   and the glory of God above,
That could come to a world of evil
   for the sake of the sinners lost,
That could drain the cup of anguish
   and never count the cost.

There is light at the cross of Jesus,
   though dark is the world around;
It was there He opened Heaven
   and the way to God was found;
It was there the tempest gathered
   and broke on His thorn-crowned head,
When He bore our stripes and sorrows,
   and suffered in our stead.

There is peace at the cross of Jesus,
   where God was reconciled,
Where we know our sins forgiven,
   and hear Him say, "My Child,"
Where He bore the world's transgressions
   and all our debt was paid,
Where the weight of the Father's anger
   on His tender heart was laid.

There is life at the cross of Jesus,
   where the victory was won,
Where sin and death were conquered
   by the sinless, deathless One;
O grave, where is thy triumph?
   O death, where is thy sting?
For the Lord of Life and Glory passed
   through thy gates a King!

- Annie Johnson Flint

Now upon the first day of the week, very early in the morning, they came unto the sepulchre, bringing the spices which they had prepared, and certain others with them. And they found the stone rolled away from the sepulchre. And they entered in, and found not the body of the Lord Jesus. And it came to pass, as they were much perplexed thereabout, behold, two men stood by them in shining garments: And as they were afraid, and bowed down their faces to the earth, they said unto them, Why seek ye the living among the dead? He is not here, but is risen . . .

St. Luke 24:1-6

The Walk to Emmaus

Late on that Easter afternoon
Two men walked down Emmaus way.
A Traveler drew near and asked,
"Why are ye sorrowful this day?"

They told Him of their Lord, condemned
Three days before, and crucified,
Yet who arose. "How can this be?"
They asked the Stranger, close beside.

He held them spellbound on the road,
As He explained the Scriptures then:
Of how God sent His Son to die,
And on the third day rose again.

At dusk they reached Emmaus, still
And peaceful in the countryside.
"The day is now far spent," they said,
"Come in and with us here abide."

And He went in that twilight hour
And sat at meat there with the two;
And as He broke and blessed the bread,
Their eyes were opened, and they knew!

Then, lo, He vanished from their sight,
And each exclaimed with one accord,
"Did not our hearts burn as He talked?
It was the Lord — our Blessed Lord!"

Immediately they rose with joy
And ran back to Jerusalem,
Telling that Jesus was alive,
And that they had communed with Him.

William Arnette Wofford

JESUS AND HIS DISCIPLES AT EMMAUS
Christen Dalsgaard
Danish, 1824-1907

The opening of the Gospel of St. Matthew - The Book of Kells

The Book of Kells

Pictured to the right is a portion of the Gospel of St. Matthew (22:11-16) from the famous *Book of Kells.* This illuminated copy of the Gospels dates from about the eighth century. Whether or not the manuscript was actually written and illuminated at the Columban monastic community in the ancient town of Kells, Ireland, is yet unsettled. The earliest reference associating the book with Kells appears in the *Annals of Ulster* for 1006. Therein it records that the Gospels were stolen from the church at Kells and subsequently found several months later buried under sod. Since 1661 the manuscript has been the chief treasure of the University Library, Trinity College, Dublin.

Authenticated News

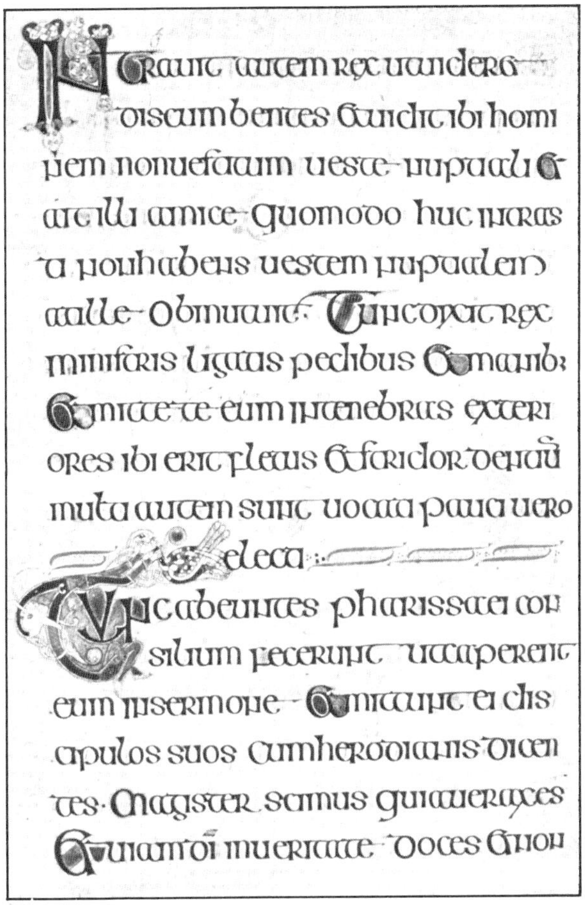

the Beatitudes

Blessed are the poor in spirit: for theirs is the kingdom of heaven.

Blessed are they that mourn: for they shall be comforted.

Blessed are the meek: for they shall inherit the earth.

Blessed are they which do hunger and thirst after righteousness: for they shall be filled.

Blessed are the merciful: for they shall obtain mercy.

Blessed are the pure in heart: for they shall see God.

Blessed are the peacemakers: for they shall be called the children of God.

Blessed are they which are persecuted for righteousness' sake: for theirs is the kingdom of heaven.

Blessed are ye, when men shall revile you, and persecute you, and shall say all manner of evil against you falsely, for my sake. Rejoice, and be exceeding glad: for great is your reward in heaven.

St. Matthew 5:3-12

Photograph opposite
Authenticated News

The Isle
of Emerald

There is an isle of the greenest green . . .
   glistening emerald, really;
Plains and fields and rolling hills
   that form the land of Eire.

O many a castle you will find,
   many a fisherman's haven,
Upon the inlets and the bays that
   form the coast of Ireland.

This is the isle of Shannon, of
   Dublin and Killarney;
Of rivers and lakes and counties fair,
   and geniuses like Shaw and O'Casey.

O this is the isle of the leprechaun,
   the shamrock and the Blarney Stone,
Where thatched-roofed cottages grace the farms
   of Ireland's charming countryside.

Here you'll find a ready wit,
   a handshake and a smile,
For the friendliest people anywhere
   live on the Emerald Isle.

Lorice Fiani Mulhern

When Erin first rose from the
　　dark-swelling flood,
God blessed the green island,
　　He saw it was good.

The Emerald of Europe,
　　it sparkled and shone
In the ring of this world,
　　the most precious stone.

William Drennan
From "Erin"

Alpha

Monastic ruins of Mellifont Abbey,
County Louth, Ireland

Thatching a roof near Lehmch,
County Clare, Ireland

Deep peace of the running wave to you,
Deep peace of the flowing air to you,
Deep peace of the quiet earth to you,
Deep peace of the shining stars to you,
Deep peace of the watching shepherds to you,
Deep peace of the Son of Peace to you.

An Old Gaelic Rune

Ralph Luedtke

A demonstration of soda bread making in the Irish booth at the Holiday Folk Fair in Milwaukee, Wisconsin

Irish Soda Bread

3¾ c. all-purpose flour
½ t. soda
½ c. sour milk
½ t. salt
½ t. cream of tartar

Mix all ingredients together except the milk. Make a well and add milk. Mix into a stiff dough. Shape into a ball. Place in a greased casserole. With a sharp knife, slash center 4 inches across and ¼-inch deep. Brush with beaten egg yolk. Bake at 350° for ¾ hour or until cake tester inserted in center comes out clean. Serve in slices. Makes 1 loaf.

Overleaf: Dooey and Horn Head, County Donegal, Ireland. Photo – Three Lions, Inc.

Traditional Irish Easter Customs

Good Friday

It was traditional never to drink milk on Good Friday. Even the baby in the cradle had to cry three times before milk was given to it.

No meat was to be hung on Good Friday, no nail driven, no wood burned and no blood shed. Cakes baked had a cross marked on them. It was considered lucky to plant seed potatoes on this day and it was believed that anyone who had their hair cut would be free of headaches for a year.

Easter Sunday

The Herring Procession

This was held following the last Mass on Easter Sunday and was usually organized by the butchers who had sold little meat during Lent. They wanted to celebrate the return of normal business by holding a mock funeral procession for a herring which symbolized abstinence. The humble herring would be dragged through town at the end of a rope, then beaten with sticks and finally tossed into the nearest stream.

The Dance of the Sun

At one time many people in all parts of Ireland held to the belief that at its rising on Easter morning, the sun could be seen dancing with joy at the Saviour's Resurrection. Children were cautioned not to look directly into the sun but rather at its reflection in a tub of water placed outside the night before. Some obliging adult would stir the water in the tub slightly so that the child would not be disappointed.

The Cake Dance

In many parts of Ireland there was a special dance held outdoors on the evening of Easter Sunday. First a cake was baked — usually boxty (made from shredded potatoes), a griddle cake, or a barley and oaten bannock. It was decorated with flowers and placed on top of a churn dash in a large field. All the courting couples of the neighborhood assembled, and the dance began. The girls danced and twirled their hoops, and the boys pounded the ground with their feet. When the dancing was over, the boy and girl dancer judged the best took the cake from the churn dash and divided it among the others. The dance was usually over before sunset. The old saying, "that takes the cake" comes from this Easter Sunday custom.

Why Eggs in Your Easter?

To most of us it's just something we do because our parents did it before us. Besides it's festive; the children enjoy colored eggs in their baskets, and it's all wrapped up with Easter somehow...

Although there is no record of eggs becoming part of the Easter celebration until the thirteenth century, the egg itself is an old symbol of new life. Ostrich eggs have been found in some early Christian graves, perhaps as a symbol of the new life in which these Christians believed.

The custom of exchanging colored eggs in spring, the season which brings new life in nature, began way back in the days of the ancient Persians and Egyptians. However, the first recorded Christians to use colored eggs were the Macedonians. They dyed most of their eggs red, the color symbolizing the blood of Christ shed on the cross. Later, red eggs became common in many countries.

During the Middle Ages in Europe the Easter liturgy included the use of a colored egg, which was placed in a representation of Jesus' tomb. Eggs used this way were sometimes decorated with gold, silver and jewels.

Today the egg rolling contests common in our land seem to have little to do with the Lord's Resurrection, but the origins of such customs can be traced to these early commemorations of the rolling away of the stone in front of Christ's tomb.

Easter egg customs are currently common in all Christian lands except Spain, Mexico and South America, where eggs seem to have little or no part in the celebration. One of the most meaningful customs comes from Germany. For many centuries many German Christians gave each other an Easter gift of three dyed eggs along with a poem.

It was the Eastern Orthodox Christians who began the practice of giving eggs as gifts on Easter morning, and they still practice this custom. Russian Orthodox Christians take their decorated eggs to the church on Easter Eve and have them blessed by the priest.

Often their eggs are still dyed red and decorated with the initial letters of the words *Khrystos voskres* (Christ is risen). In Greece, Orthodox Church members use such symbols as the Chi-Rho, the two opening letters in Greek of the name Christ.

Russians and Greeks still observe the custom of presenting these eggs with the greeting "Christ is risen!" to which the one who receives it replies, "He is risen indeed!"

Some churches have borrowed these words from the Orthodox liturgy for their own Easter services. The service begins with the pastor's proclamation, "Christ is risen!" and the congregation's joyful response, "He is risen indeed!"

Whether or not that old, stirring Easter greeting has been part of your liturgical tradition, you might consider making the Orthodox egg customs part of your Easter tradition. Have a reason for dyeing and giving eggs at Easter. Let them proclaim the Resurrection of Christ! Paint on them a Chi-Rho, an Alleluia, a Pax (Peace), or a fish. And let them express your renewal of life, faith and love through the ever-living Lord and Savior.

Alice Stolper Peppler

the sun, the moon and the rooster

A Slovakian Easter Legend

Down through the ages people have commemorated in festival and story the reawakening of nature in the spring. The legend about the sun, the moon and the rooster dates from pagan times in old Slovakia, but like other cherished myths and traditions, has become a part of the Slovakian celebration of Easter. The story is told to children shortly before Easter as the traditional decorations are placed on an Easter egg tree similar to the one shown on the opposite page.

One day the sun and the moon and a little rooster went out walking. The sun said to the moon, "Why don't you and the rooster look after the sheep for a while?" and nodded toward the stars that studded the sky. The moon was lazy and left the job to the rooster. But the rooster was too weak and the star-sheep were in a tangle.

Angered, the moon seized the rooster by its bright red comb and threw him to the earth.

So today the rooster is always afraid of the moon. He calls his family up on the tree in the late afternoon, and early in the morning he shouts to tell the world he is glad his friend the sun is coming back.

The beautiful Slovakian egg tree in the photograph is one of the many ways Christians around the world mark the celebration of Easter. Over two hundred exquisitely decorated eggshells, symbolic of the Resurrection of Christ, are used in the construction of the tree. Other decorations include colored ribbons signifying the four seasons, pussy willows, blossoms and three objects representing the characters in the old Slovakian legend.

Photograph opposite
SLOVAKIAN EGG TREE
Egg tree and legend above
courtesy of Mrs. Stefan Biksadski,
Milwaukee, Wisconsin
Photo – Ralph Luedtke

A Bunny Tale

Two bunnies went a-hopping
To find a "bunny store."
Their mother sent them shopping
With thoughts of Easter lore.

In windows they were peeking
All up and down the street.
They found what they were seeking
In a gift shop, bright and neat.

They saw Miss Fluff designing
With paints of every hue;
Their bunny eyes were shining
As she held an egg of blue.

At samples they were looking
And deciding what to buy;
They needed pots for cooking
And envelopes of dye.

They needed straw for lacing
The baskets they would make;
Some patterns, too, for tracing
And jellybeans for cake.

Now homeward they were going
With tired bunny legs
When they remembered knowing
They should have bought some eggs!

Maude G. Booth

Easter Is a Blessing

Easter is a memory time...
Of colored eggs and pretty dresses,
Of yellow chicks and curly tresses.

Easter is a renewing time...
For baby bunnies, birds and bees,
For sun and rain on budding trees.

Easter is a grateful time...
For all our blessings every day,
For health and friends along the way.

Easter is a believing time...
That Christ arose for us to see
The way to grow eternally.

Easter is a joyful time...
For thoughts, for growth, for songs to sing.
Yes, Easter is a constant spring.

Ruth Carrington

EASTER GREETINGS

The flowers lend their colors
Of every varied hue
To brighten up the Easter wish
That Bunny paints for you.

An Easter postcard from the early 1900's. The custom of sending Easter greetings by picture postcard originated in Germany and became popular in the United States in the 1870's. The vogue lasted until about 1910 when present-day greeting cards with envelopes became more widely used.

Ralph Luedtke

The Tale of Peter Rabbit's Creator

Harrison E. Salisbury

Beatrix Potter in 1943

On September 4, 1893, a year distinguished by such events as a panic in Wall Street, the Chicago Columbian Exposition and the closing days of Gladstone's long consulship, a rather shy, almost dowdy twenty-seven-year-old English woman sat down at her desk and wrote a letter to five-year-old Noel Carter.

"My dear Noel," the letter began. "I don't know what to write to you, so I shall tell you a story about four little rabbits, whose names were Flopsy, Mopsy, Cottontail and Peter.

"They lived with their mother in a sandbank under the root of a big fir tree.

" 'Now, my dears,' said old Mrs. Bunny, 'you may go into the field or down the lane, but, don't go into Mr. McGregor's garden . . .' "

In between the paragraphs the writer drew delicately lined sketches of Flopsy, Mopsy, Cottontail and all the rest.

And so the saga began — the incredible tale of Peter Rabbit and some thirty-three other tales, collections and fairy stories written by Beatrix Potter before her death on December 22, 1943 at the age of seventy-seven.

If the opening words of that long ago letter to little Noel Carter reverberate in the minds of millions

Cover design by Beatrix Potter.
Used through courtesy of
Frederick Warne & Co., Inc.

here in America, in England and around the world — it is no accident. For the tale which Miss Potter spun to amuse her little friend and the illustrations she drew across the letter pages were transferred almost unchanged to the tale of Peter Rabbit which has never gone out of print since 1901 when Miss Potter hesitantly published it at her own expense in an edition of 250 copies.

Frederick Warne & Co., the quiet, rather old-fashioned English publishing firm which became Miss Potter's publisher, cannot say how many million copies of "Peter Rabbit" and her other books have sold over the last sixty-odd years. But twenty-six of her titles, including twenty-three of the basic stories like "Peter Rabbit," the "Tale of Two Bad Mice" and the "Tale of Pigling Bland," are still in print.

What of the creator of these wonderful, enduring tales?

In Margaret Lane's charming biography, "The Tale of Beatrix Potter," Miss Lane recreates for us in bright and lively hues the Victorian world which shaped Miss Potter's character and stimulated her genius; the solitary childhood, the long hours of observation of beetles, toadstools, caterpillars, foxglove, snapdragons, sage and pinks; the specimens and dissections; the sketching and painting

of flowers; the museum study of fossils and embroidery; the unbroken routine of well-to-do middle class social life, winters at Bolton Gardens, in London; summers in the lake country, Scotland, watering places; the round of visits to aunts and cousins by the dozens.

In this unlikely atmosphere Miss Potter's cool, unexpected imagination bore sudden fruit. Her tales and drawings, inimitably interconnected, were published and won fantastic popularity over the stubborn and consistent opposition of her conventional parents.

In the first decade after 1900 an incredible succession of tales spilled from Miss Potter's deft hand and mind. Then, nearly fifty, she married (her rash act in wedding a country barrister caused a family row worthy of the most melodramatic conceits of the Brontë sisters).

The remarkable creative well swiftly ran dry. Indeed, no longer did she really care about Peter Rabbit, Tom Kitten, Jemima Puddle-Duck and all the rest. She plunged into a second career which occupied the remaining years of her life — that of a sturdy north country farming woman, as intent and skillful at managing her Berwick sheep as in an earlier day she had been in inventing the anthropomorphic mice, rats, cats, bunnies and foxes which populate her tales.

Why are the Beatrix Potter stories classic?

"They are good art," is the simple and accurate answer of Miss Lane. She recalls Lord David Cecil's statement about Dickens: "It does not matter that Dickens' world is not lifelike; it is alive."

So it is with the animal world which Beatrix Potter created.

The Tale of Peter Rabbit

Beatrix Potter

Once upon a time there were four little rabbits, and their names were Flopsy, Mopsy, Cottontail and Peter.

They lived with their mother in a sandbank, underneath the root of a very big fir tree.

"Now, my dears," said old Mrs. Rabbit one morning, "you may go into the fields or down the lane, but don't go into Mr. McGregor's garden: your father met with an accident there; he was put in a pie by Mrs. McGregor. Now run along, and don't get into mischief. I am going out."

Then old Mrs. Rabbit took a basket and her umbrella, and went through the woods to the baker's. She bought a loaf of bread and five currant buns.

Flopsy, Mopsy and Cottontail, who were good little bunnies, went down the lane to gather blackberries; but Peter, who was very naughty, ran straight away to Mr. McGregor's garden, and squeezed under the gate! First he ate some lettuces and some French beans; and then he ate some radishes; and then, feeling rather sick, he went to look for some parsley.

But round the end of a cucumber frame, whom should he meet but Mr. McGregor.

Mr. McGregor was on his hands and knees planting out young cabbages, but he jumped up and ran after Peter, waving a rake and calling out, "Stop thief!"

Peter was most dreadfully frightened; he rushed all over the garden, for he had forgotten the way back to the gate. He lost one of his shoes among the cabbages, and the other shoe amongst the potatoes.

After losing them, he ran on four legs, and went faster, so that I think he might have gotten away altogether, if he had not unfortunately run into a gooseberry net, and got caught by the large buttons on his jacket. It was a blue jacket with brass buttons, quite new.

Peter gave himself up for lost, and shed big tears; but his sobs were overheard by some friendly sparrows, who flew to him in great excitement, and implored him to exert himself.

Continued

Mr. McGregor came up with a sieve, which he intended to pop upon the top of Peter; but Peter wriggled out just in time, leaving his jacket behind him.

He rushed into the toolshed, and jumped into a can. It would have been a beautiful thing to hide in, if it had not had so much water in it.

Mr. McGregor was quite sure that Peter was somewhere in the toolshed, perhaps hidden underneath a flowerpot. He began to turn them over carefully, looking under each.

Presently Peter sneezed — "Kertyschoo!" Mr. McGregor was after him in no time, and tried to put his foot upon Peter, who jumped out the window, upsetting three plants. The window was too small for Mr. McGregor, and he was tired of running after Peter. He went back to his work.

Peter sat down to rest; he was out of breath and trembling with fright, and he had not the least idea which way to go. Also he was very damp with sitting in that can.

After a time he began to wander about, going lippity-lippity not very fast, and looking all around.

He found a door in a wall; but it was locked, and there was no room for a fat little rabbit to squeeze underneath.

An old mouse was running in and out over the stone doorstep, carrying peas and beans to her family in the wood. Peter asked her the way to the gate, but she had such a large pea in her mouth that she could not answer. She only shook her head at him. Peter began to cry.

Then he tried to find his way straight across the garden, but he became more and more puzzled. Presently he came to a pond where Mr. McGregor filled his watercans. A white cat was staring at some goldfish; she sat very, very still, but now and then, the tip of her tail twitched as if it were alive. Peter thought it best to go away without speaking to her; he had heard about cats from his cousin, little Benjamin Bunny.

He went back toward the toolshed, but suddenly, quite close to him, he heard the noise of a hoe — scr-r-ritch, scratch, scratch, scritch. Peter scuttered underneath the bushes. But presently, as nothing happened, he came out, and climbed upon a wheelbarrow and peeped over. The first thing that he saw was Mr. McGregor hoeing onions. His back was turned toward Peter, and beyond him was the gate.

Peter got down very quietly off the wheelbarrow, and started running as fast as he could go, along a straight walk behind some black currant bushes.

Mr. McGregor caught sight of him at the corner, but Peter did not care. He slipped underneath the gate, and was safe at last in the woods outside the garden.

Mr. McGregor hung up the little jacket and the shoes for a scarecrow to frighten the blackbirds.

Peter never stopped running or looked behind him till he got home to the big fir tree.

He was so tired that he flopped down upon the nice soft sand on the floor of the rabbit hole and shut his eyes. His mother was busy cooking; she wondered what he had done with his clothes. It was the second little jacket and pair of shoes that Peter had lost in a fortnight!

I am sorry to say that Peter was not very well during the evening.

His mother put him to bed, and made some camomile tea; and she gave a dose of it to Peter!

"One tablespoonful to be taken at bedtime."

But Flopsy, Mopsy and Cottontail had bread and milk and blackberries for supper.

Rain Flowers

School children go hurrying by
Under weeping skies of grey,
And their bobbing umbrellas
Color-splash the rainy day;

Blue, pink, yellow, purple, orange,
Flower-patterned, striped and plain,
Mingle, part and then re-cluster,
Bright blossoms dancing in the rain.

Laughing faces half revealed
By tilting umbrellas gay . . .
There's joy in watching flowers that bloom
Only on a rainy day.

Marjorie Helmer

Silver April Rain

The silver rain of April
Wakes every bush and tree,
And coaxes green buds forth
To bloom in ecstasy.

It dances on the rooftops
And up and down each pane;
It marches on the pavements
And patters down the lane.

It makes the sweetest music
Like a happy song of spring,
'Tis a merry little mischief,
Refreshing everything.

Raincoats and umbrellas
Are used throughout its stay,
And it leaves a brilliant rainbow
As silver droplets steal away.

April rain is but a promise
Of spring's beauty and delight,
So enjoy its silver goodness,
Before it fades from sight.

LaVerne P. Larson

*Photograph opposite
Alpha*

from the editor's scrapbook

Spring . . . it is a natural resurrection;
an experience of immortality.

Thoreau

The great Easter truth is not that we are to live
newly after death — that is not the great thing —
but that we are to be new here and now by the
power of the resurrection; not so much that we are
to live forever as that we are to, and may, live
nobly now because we are to live forever.

Phillips Brooks

The message of Easter is one of assurance,
of joy, and of triumph.

Author Unknown

There's a path that leads through
a woodland —
A path that I love to trod,
To get away from this wide world's rush
And be alone with God.

Author Unknown

Nature gives to every time and season some
beauties of its own; and from morning to night, as
from the cradle to the grave, is but a succession of
changes so gentle and easy that we can scarcely
mark their progress.

Charles Dickens

The year's at the spring, and the day's
at the morn;
Morning's at seven; the hillside's
dew-pearled;
The lark's on the wing; the snail's on
the thorn;
God's in His heaven — all's right with
the world!

Robert Browning

Easter is an awakening of every living thing. A time
when soul and spirits rise, as heaven receives
its King.

Olive Dunkelberger

He that has no cross will have no crown.

Quarles

Shadow and sunshine, clouds, then blue skies;
Soft new grass carpet underfoot lies;
Flowers a-blooming, budding green leaves;
Bees making honey, birds' nests near the eaves . . .
All signs of promise spring's on the way,
Ready to welcome a bright Easter Day.

Emma E. Kinne

I know not where His islands lift
Their fronded palms in air;
I only know I cannot drift
Beyond His love and care.

John Greenleaf Whittier

A gush of birdsong, a patter of dew,
A cloud, and a rainbow's warning,
Suddenly sunshine and perfect blue...
An April day in the morning.

Harriet Prescott Spofford

People are like stained glass windows. They glow and sparkle when it is sunny and bright; but when the sun goes down their true beauty is revealed only if there is a light from within.

Author Unknown

Life's sweetest joys are hidden in unsubstantial things: an April rain, a fragrance, a vision of blue wings.

M. R. Smith

I think of the garden after the rain,
And hope to my heart comes singing,
"At morn the cherry blooms will be white,
And the Easter bells be ringing!"

Edna Dean Procter

What is lovely never dies,
But passes into other loveliness,
Stardust, or seafoam, flower
or winged air.

Thomas A. Aldrich

We are only certain of today... yesterday is gone and tomorrow is always coming.

Martin Vanbee

O Lord, our Lord, how excellent is thy name in all the earth! who hast set thy glory above the heavens. When I consider thy heavens, the work of thy fingers, the moon and the stars, which thou has ordained: What is man, that thou art mindful of him?

Psalm 8:1, 3-4

Stronger than the dark, the light;
Stronger than the wrong, the right;
Faith and hope triumphant say
Christ will rise on Easter Day.

Phillips Brooks

Arise, go thy way: thy faith hath made thee whole.

Luke 17:19

Peace I leave with you, my peace I give unto you: not as the world giveth, give I unto you. Let not your heart be troubled, neither let it be afraid.

John 14:27

Take a Journey of Love

James C. Pippin

As a spiritual adventure during Lent (or for any period in the year), I suggest you take a special six-week trip. You won't need extra clothes, there won't be much travel involved, nor will you have to spend a lot of money.

The preparation will be mostly in your spirit, and pens, paper and Bible are recommended aids.

FIRST WEEK: *The Hand of Love*

Write a letter a day to a friend, someone not related to you, near or faraway. Tell them how much you appreciate them.

SECOND WEEK: *The Voice of Love*

Telephone two or three people each day for a short chat, just to say what they mean to you or to say "Thank you" or "I'm sorry." Call people you have intended to phone but somehow never have.

THIRD WEEK: *The Deed of Love*

Take something you have made or bought to two or three friends who mean a lot to you, but for whom you rarely express your love — a pie, plant, apron, a small remembrance that has your love as a wrapping.

FOURTH WEEK: *The Heart of Love*

Make a list of at least ten people for whom you will pray daily. Include your friends, your enemies, those you don't particularly like. Forgive them if they have wronged you, and ask forgiveness if you have wronged them.

FIFTH WEEK: *The Mind of Love*

Use this week to pray for yourself and look inward. Read the book of John. Plan to go to church early on Palm Sunday, to meditate in the sanctuary.

SIXTH WEEK: *The Victory of Love*

This is the week of celebration. God's love for us is revealed in many ways. Get outdoors and breathe in the air of spring. Have friends in for dinner and games. Let your joy be full with life abundant in faith, hope and love.

Reprinted by permission from GUIDEPOSTS MAGAZINE, Copyright 1974 by Guideposts Associates, Inc., Carmel, New York 10512.

Mother's Yellow Easter Dress

While glancing through the album, an old one I confess,
I saw my mother's picture, taken in her yellow Easter dress.
How well I can remember when she wore it, many years ago . . .
A vision of loveliness, her features all aglow.

She had fashioned it with loving care, and sewn for several weeks
To achieve that chic perfection, which every woman seeks.
She refused to let us see it, for it wasn't even worn
Until she made her entrance down the stairs that Easter morn.

We were standing there, just waiting, in our Sunday Easter best,
Even Father stood there quietly, but suspenseful as the rest.
His blue eyes never wavered, and a smile lit up his face
When Mother started downward at her usual graceful pace.

We stared in childish wonder as she stopped at Father's side,
For Mother walked in beauty . . . every heart filled up with pride.
The golden trim of ribbon and the lace so creamy white
Gave her yellow dress an elegance of Easter time delight.

I'm glad I saw that certain picture of my mother once again,
Because it brought back memories of happy times; but then,
I never do regret the time it takes to sit and look
At old and treasured albums . . . they're a picture storybook.

J. Evelyn Smith

When Spring Has Come Again

When spring has come again I'll go back home,
Where blossoming orchards stretch like waves of foam
As far as eye can see;
Where meadows green embrace the shining brook,
Where groves of maples flaunt their brightest look
And seem to welcome me.

I'll see the old red barn, and then recall
The fun its hayloft held for one and all
When we were young and gay;
Beneath the chestnut tree, beside the lane,
That sparkled after being drenched with rain,
Was our favorite place to play.

But most of all, my loved ones I'll behold,
As once again I enter in the fold
Of warmth that happy day,
To laugh with joy, to share the festive board
And all the wondrous memories to hoard,
When springtime comes this way.

Eleanor J. Elkins

Photograph opposite
REFLECTING POND
near Roxbury, Wisconsin
Photo – Ken Dequaine

Spring Plowing

He walks the furrow's narrow way,
And measures off with sweet content
The land that glows before his eyes
With warm and pulsing wonderment;
For spring now flaunts its apple-green
On meadowland and leafing boughs,
And delights the very heart and soul
Of one who guides the moving plow.

Above the horses' plodding hoofs,
Sweeps the shrill, transcendent call
Of a meadowlark that finds delight
In trilling forth its song to all;
And as the plowshare cuts its way
Through the warm and fragrant earth,
The farmer feels a joy and closeness
With the season springing into birth.

Enlivened by the morning air,
The woodsy scent from yonder grove,
He carefully turns his sturdy plow
And treads the furrow of another row;
While April's young and stirring breeze
Wafts gently past his cheek,
And ripples through the snowy crown
Of dogwood trees down by the creek.

About him lies his wealth and joy,
The fertile sod beneath his feet,
The beauty of the field and sky,
The glow of spring, fragrant and sweet...
And he walks the furrow's way
Content, from all the world apart,
With the meadowlark's sweet lilting call
Still echoing within his heart!

Joy Belle Burgess

Downy Things

Glenn Ward Dresbach

First of the downy things to wake and stir
Are pussy willows, matched like fuzzy pearls,
Then maple buds, across the smoky blur
Of branches on the sky, from which unfurls
The first slow banner. Over boulders moss
Then spreads its soft-stitched mantle, and the plush
Is on the young buck's horns; wild ducklings cross,
Like fluffy balls, the water's silver hush.

By farms, chicks soon are feeding in the sun
And kittens roll in doorways touched with gold.
Too soon the cottonwoods, where floss is spun,
Will lose it all. The looms of wind will hold
The milkweed floss, the last of downy things . . .
When blue haze trembles with departing wings.

Photograph opposite
Pat Powers

Lavender Lilacs

Have you ever breathed the fragrance
   of a lilac bush in bloom?
Then you'll not forget the pleasure
   of its dewy fresh perfume.

There were lilacs in the dooryard
   of the home where I was born.
Mother cut bouquets of lilacs
   in the coolness of the morn.

There are lilacs in my dooryard,
   planted many years ago,
By a flower-loving mother
   whose hands helped roots to grow.

Bushes of lavender lilacs,
   bouquets of fragrant perfume,
May the lilacs in the dooryards
   never cease to yield their bloom!

Jeannette K. Olson

When Lilacs Bloom

When I was just a little girl, I wondered why in spring
My mother couldn't stay inside to finish anything.
She'd take a wide-brimmed hat and gloves, a rake, her special hoe,
And string and stakes and packs of seeds, and singing softly, go
To where she loved to spend those precious first spring hours,
Where working hand-in-hand with God, she dreamed of summer flowers.

I longed to help, but could not curb that special ecstasy
That spring brought to the bright young world of little girls like me.
How could my mother kneel so long to plant those tiny seeds
And later hour by dreary hour sort beauty from the weeds,
When I could only run and play and revel in blue sky,
The scent of lilacs, willow's gold and breezes whispering by.

But now that I am grown I know the magic of the row,
Where Mother didn't call it "work" to tend with rake and hoe
The little plot she leased from God the while she traveled here.
She found a special peace and joy and in springtime every year,
And when the lilacs bloom in spring... their fragrance everywhere...
I love my little garden plot and feel her presence there.

Harriet Elmblad

The Wild Ones

The woodlands now awake again
   with nature's symphony,
As wildlife knows it's spring again,
   in perfect harmony
The little creatures venture forth,
   the birds in rapture sing,
And down the greening aisles they flit
   on bright, ecstatic wing.

Wake-robin lifts its petaled head,
   the violets arise,
Jack-in-the-pulpit comes to preach
   his praises to the skies.
Anemone its white blooms sway,
   arbutus lifts its face,
While squirrels cavort at their play
   beneath wild plum tree lace.

The little rabbit hops in glee,
   the chipmunk scampers by
A spotted fawn we may not see
   in mottled leaves nearby,
And if we look most carefully
   neath a toadstool parasol,
Perhaps an elfman we might see,
   he, too, hears springtime's call.

The sun through green casts dappled shade
   where whispering footsteps go
On journeys through the forest glade
   with language we can't know,
But in our hearts we understand
   both man and wild ones hear
The same sweet voice upon the land,
   released from woe or fear,
Rejoice again as warmth seeps in
   to wake the earth below
And at dusk in fern-edged pool trills
   the frog's gay tremolo.

Ruth B. Field

Photograph opposite
Arnout Hyde, Jr.

The High Country

Harry Noyes Pratt

It's blossom time in the high country,
  Where the slender aspens grow,
    And the lilies peep
    From the boulder heap
  At the edge of the melting snow.

It's blossom time in the high country,
  Where a thousand banners fling
    Their thundering spray
    To the gleaming day
  As the flying waters sing.

It's blossom time in the high country,
  Gay with a thousand blooms;
    Where the daisy's cup
    Comes smiling up,
  And the larkspur lifts its plumes.

When it's blossom time on the mountainside,
  Then the hills are calling me
    Through the shimmering day
    To the hill highway . . .
  I'm off for the high country!

Morning in April

The spring is tender in the woods today,
The sky an arching bow from rim to rim
Above an April world and birds convey
A blithesome promise from each greening limb.

The flowering trees are little puffs of light
Against the rich, green velvet of the grass;
This April morning opens to invite
Wild flowers out along the way I pass.

Filled with new life the trees lift arms to pray
For spring is tender in the woods today.

Helen Virden

Summer Is Coming

On a day in early spring, when the woods are bare and the fields brown, when the earth is mantled with gray clouds and chilled with raw mist, we ask, "Where is the summer that was promised?" But looking closer, we see upon the orchards a faint flush of springing buds, and on sheltered hillsides the grass is green; under the dead leaves we may find the arbutus, and now and then the note of a bluebird pierces the air. Summer is coming! And God's summer is coming among men. Not tomorrow, perhaps, nor next year, but in His good time. Surer than the apple blossoms of next June, fairer than the brightest day on which the sun ever rose.

C. S. Merriam

*Photographs opposite:
spring forest scene by
H. Armstrong Roberts;
arbutus by Gottscho-
Schleisner*

For the Beauty of the Earth

Kathleen Blanchard

The story behind a best-loved hymn...

Folliott Sandford Pierpoint was born at Bath, England, 1825. He was sent to the famous school founded by Edward VI for free education "for worthie scholars" — Bath Grammar School. In due course he went on to Queen's College, Oxford.

After taking his degree, he took up scholastic work at Somersetshire College, an educational center in the west of England. But as the years passed, literary work called him away from schoolwork, except for the coaching of private pupils.

He published several works from his seaside home in Devon, including "The Chalice of Nature and Other Poems." He also wrote a number of lyrics which were published.

But the hymn by which he is remembered is the one below. It was written while the author was staying with friends in the city that held him most — Bath.

One day in late spring when he was about twenty-nine, he had rambled down lanes where the bank was covered with sweet-scented violets, the primroses were peeping from between their leaves, and all the earth seemed glad. He then climbed the hill nearby and sat to rest. Entranced by the view that lay before him, under the spell of the beauty of it all — Bath, the countryside, hill and vale, the winding river Avon in the distance, the lovely sky with groups of billowing white clouds across the heavens — his heart welled up with emotion and he expressed with his pen the feelings that were within him in the following hymn:

For the beauty of the earth,
For the beauty of the skies,
For the love which from our birth,
Over and around us lies,
Lord of all, to Thee we raise,
This our sacrifice of praise.

For the beauty of each hour,
Of the day and of the night,
Hill and vale, and tree and flower,
Sun and moon, and stars of light,
Lord of all, to Thee we raise,
This our sacrifice of praise.

For the joy of ear and eye,
For the heart and mind's delight,
For the mystic harmony
Linking sense to sound and sight,
Lord of all, to Thee we raise,
This our sacrifice of praise.

For the joy of human love,
Brother, sister, parent, child,
Friends on earth and friends above,
For all gentle thoughts and mild,
Lord of all, to Thee we raise,
This our sacrifice of praise.

For each perfect gift of Thine
To our race so freely given,
Graces human and divine,
Flowers of earth and buds of Heaven,
Lord of all, to Thee we raise,
This our sacrifice of praise.

Folliott Sandford Pierpoint

April Fires

Golden poppy growing wild,
The desert's bright and lovely child.

Signature of God's design
Where cacti rears its bitter spine.

Gilding plains that barren lie
Beneath the desert's lonely sky.

Bursting from the heart of spring
Yellow blossoms quivering.

Red rocks crowned with golden spires
The desert's dazzling April fires.

Breathless wonder to all men,
The desert sings of God again.

Dorothy Evelyn Begg

Holy Week

The desert touched my soul...
I know I will not forget
Its awesomeness, its beauty,
Its mountains and its valley
Strewn with flowers of gold;
The birds that love its mesquite,
Its cactus and its sage;
The sunset that so changes all the earth;
That first star in the deep blue sky;
The moon that hangs down low;
The desert touched my soul...
I know I will not forget
That when the fragrant perfumes rise,
Like sacerdotal incense from the earth,
My soul uplifted found a paradise.
Then, came tranquillity and peace.
I met God face-to-face.

Margaret Drake Elliott

Photograph opposite
THE DESERT IN SPRING
Photo – Tom Stack and
Associates by William Eastman III

MY HEART IS HIGH

My heart is high with meadowlarks,
   my heart is winging hills;
My heart is where the tallest trees
   touch heaven's windowsills.

My heart is wide with rainbow fields,
   my heart draws rivers in;
My heart is reaching, stretching far
   where ocean shores begin.

My heart is deep with daffodils,
   my heart has songs to sing;
My heart is deep, my heart is wide,
   my heart is high with spring.

Maurice Hill

Reprinted by permission of William Morrow & Co. from TED
MALONE'S ADVENTURES IN POETRY. Copyright © 1946
by William Morrow & Co.

Where
Nature
Walks

Where nature walks my feet would go
To country lanes where violets grow,
A distant hill, a meadow green,
A flowing brook I've not yet seen,
A golden sun, a sky of blue
With fluffy clouds a-stealing through.

Where nature walks I shall find peace;
'Tis here that beauty doth increase
The lovely things, the music sweet,
Where hope and faith are more complete,
A mountaintop my heart would trod . . .
'Tis here I shall commune with God.

Where nature walks — no crowded place —
'Tis here life wears a happy face,
A time to work, a time to rest,
A place to find the very best,
With promise rich we might fulfill
The quiet time of being still.

We hear a breeze — oh, gentle sound —
And pause to touch the warming ground,
The friendly hills, the valley fair,
Someday I'd like to take you there . . .
The world alive where springtime stalks
To thrill a heart, where nature walks.

Garnett Ann Schultz

Star cactus in bloom

On That Desert Countryside

Out among the desert mesas,
   Christ, the Master, hid away,
Finding solitude and refuge
   Where He went to fast and pray.

When the evening solace deepened
   As the shadows crossed His path,
And the heady air of twilight,
   Like a blessed aftermath,
Filled His body, soothed His spirit
   As He walked the desert ways,
Did He find there, humble creatures
   That could share His lonely days?

Were there tiny desert rabbits,
   Or strange lizards, sleepy-eyed?
Were there herds of small wild burros
   On that desert countryside?
Did He watch their friendly antics,
   Smiling kindly; could He see
That upon a humble burro
   He would ride toward Calvary?

Lorraine Ussher Babbitt

God's Corner

The delicate fragrance of Easter lilies! The roll and ebb of resonant organ music! The stirring cadences of the velvet-tongued man of God as he interprets the Easter message! The dramatic crescendo of the choir as it rises to a climax in a final "He is risen!"

The congregation stirs. The spell is broken. The Resurrection has been commemorated for another year. One passes on to more mundane matters.

For nature, the resurrection is less dramatic but perhaps more meaningful. By the third week of the new year, ravens and owls appear in pairs in the forest. They are searching for suitable trees in which to build their nests. They are very selective in their choice. Ravens usually build in pine trees. Owls prefer the hardwoods . . . crotches of yellow birch or maples. By late February or early March new life erupts in those nests, and the resurrection of spring is on the way.

Another sign of nature's restoration of vigor is found at the base of trees. There may be three or four feet of snow on the ground and temperatures may be freezing, but gradually at the base of a tree the snow begins to recede. Says the forester, "That means spring is on the way." And what is spring but the resurrection of nature.

One of the most subtle indications of early change in nature's thinking is a gray shadow that appears on snow-covered areas. It is as though the heavens had sprayed dust with a lavish hand. Underneath those gray areas water is building up that before too long will surface. Shelley knew whereof he spoke when he concluded his ode to the west wind with, "O wind, if winter comes, can spring be far behind?"

Where do you and I stand in this matter of resurrection? Are we living in a rut that is slowly engulfing us? Are we steeped in traditional yesterdays? Or are we joyously living the resurrection in our daily lives because we are teeming with resurrected thought?

If we were to define "resurrected thought" would it not be thought that was revitalized by the strength of an unshakeable faith in the omnipresence and omnipotence of the Father within us? Compromise is a popular fallacy. Resurrection is the lifting of consciousness from the tomb of lost hopes to the aliveness of spiritual entity.

Do we not mistakenly associate the Nazarene carpenter only with His Resurrection from the tomb when in reality His entire mission was one of resurrection? His directives were simple and yet replete with restoration of vigor: "Take up thy bed and walk;" "Lazarus, come forth;" "Go, and sin no more;" "Be of good comfort, thy faith hath made thee whole."

What an influence for good you and I could be in a world sadly in need of good, were we to release the pent-up repressions that torment us and instead, rejoice in the peaceful security of a renewed and revitalized consciousness. That would be our resurrection.

Gertrude M. Puelicher

A Lifted Trumpet Sounds

Across the ramparts of eternity
A lifted trumpet sounds this Easter hour,
To reassure all eager listening hearts
That truly the Christ is risen, that no power
Could have stayed the rock that sealed His sepulcher;
Could have stilled the voice that sounds upon the air:
Joining the true bright trumpet notes until
They can be heard to the world's far everywhere.

"I am the resurrection and the life,
He that believeth in me . . . shall never die.
Because I live ye shall live also," the voice
And the silver trumpet notes sound down the sky!
A duet from the far eternal shore —
A blessed Christ, we shout our praise to Thee
For this holy day, and for Thy continuing voice
With its glorious promise of immortality.

Grace Noll Crowell

Photograph opposite
Fred Sieb

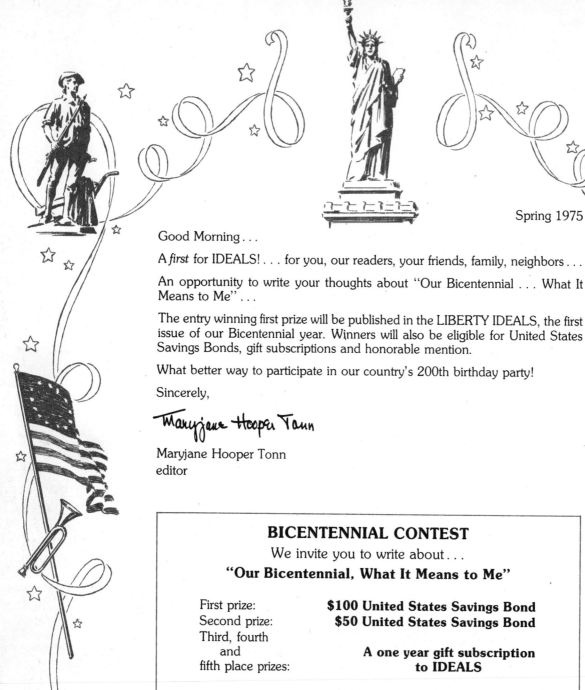

Spring 1975

Good Morning . . .

A *first* for IDEALS! . . . for you, our readers, your friends, family, neighbors . . .

An opportunity to write your thoughts about "Our Bicentennial . . . What It Means to Me" . . .

The entry winning first prize will be published in the LIBERTY IDEALS, the first issue of our Bicentennial year. Winners will also be eligible for United States Savings Bonds, gift subscriptions and honorable mention.

What better way to participate in our country's 200th birthday party!

Sincerely,

Maryjane Hooper Tonn

Maryjane Hooper Tonn
editor

BICENTENNIAL CONTEST
We invite you to write about . . .
"Our Bicentennial, What It Means to Me"

First prize:	**$100 United States Savings Bond**
Second prize:	**$50 United States Savings Bond**
Third, fourth and fifth place prizes:	**A one year gift subscription to IDEALS**

CONTEST RULES Entries must be: 1. A prose essay in your own words on the following theme: "Our Bicentennial, What It Means to Me." 2. Typewritten, double-spaced, or printed legibly. 3. 250 words or less in length. 4. Original material not previously submitted to or published in another publication. 5. Clearly marked with name and address of author. 6. Addressed to "Bicentennial Contest" c/o Ideals Publishing Corp., 11315 Watertown Plank Road, Milwaukee, Wisconsin 53226. 7. Postmarked no later than midnight on July 30, 1975. 8. Entries cannot be returned. 9. Entries will be judged for originality and creativity by the editorial staff of the Ideals Publishing Corp. Judges' decision will be considered final. 10. Winners will be notified by mail no later than October 31, 1975. 11. Employees of the Ideals Publishing Corp. or their relatives are not eligible.

Acknowledgments: *A LIFTED TRUMPET SOUNDS by Grace Noll Crowell. From LET THE SUN SHINE IN by Grace Noll Crowell. Copyright © 1970 by Fleming H. Revell Company. Used by permission. DOWNY THINGS by Glenn Ward Dresbach. Reprinted with permission from THE SATURDAY EVENING POST, © 1938 The Curtis Publishing Company. LORD OF US ALL by Donald Hankey. From MASTERPIECES OF RELIGIOUS VERSE. Reprinted by permission of Harper & Row, Publishers. FROM NAZARETH HE COMES by Raymond Kresensky. Copyright Christian Century Foundation. Reprinted by permission from THE CHRISTIAN CENTURY. THE ISLE OF EMERALD by Lorice Fiani Mulhern. From REALMS OF ENCHANTMENT by Lorice Fiani Mulhern. Copyright © 1970 by Lorice Fiani Mulhern. Published by Dorrance & Company. WHY EGGS IN YOUR EASTER by Alice Stolper Peppler, from THE LUTHERAN WITNESS, Volume 93, No. 5 (April 7, 1974). Reprinted by permission of Concordia Publishing House. THE COMING OF SPRING by Nora Perry. From THE HOME BOOK OF VERSE FOR YOUNG FOLKS published by Houghton Mifflin Company. THE TALE OF PETER RABBIT by Beatrix Potter reproduced by permission of the publisher, Frederick Warne & Company, Inc. GOD'S CORNER by Gertrude M. Puelicher. Previously published in EXCLUSIVELY YOURS, April 1974. AN EASTER SONG by Christina G. Rossetti. From SING-SONG by Christina G. Rossetti, published by Macmillan Publishing Co., Inc. Our sincere thanks to the following author whose address we were unable to locate for material in this book: Elinor Lennen for HIS LAST WEEK.*

Additional photo credits: *Front and back covers by Ralph Luedtke. Inside covers by Fred Sieb.*